Date Due

MAR 8	DEC 19 1991		June 7
	MAY 5 1992		
APR 09 1985			
MAR. 16 1989	FEB. 24 1989		
JAN 10 1990	Staff		
DEC 1 4 1990	FEB 04 1995		
Staff	JUN 5 1996		
NOV 26 1997	R.B		
MAR 18 1998	MAR 1 5 2001		
Staff			

c. 1

942.08
DAV

Davies, Penelope
  Children of the
industrial revolution.

About this book

The Industrial Revolution was a time of great change in England. New machines were invented and factories were built. Many families left the countryside and came to the cities to work in the factories and mills. All the pictures in this book were drawn or painted more than a hundred years ago. They will show you what life was like for working children during the Industrial Revolution.

Here are pictures of children working in mines and factories, going to ragged schools, and coming home to the terrible slums where so many families had to live. You can also read what people living at the time wrote and said. Some of the eyewitnesses were the children themselves, who were forced to work long hours at dreary tasks. Others were grownups who tried to improve the children's lives. Look carefully at these pages and you will find out how many children really lived in the 19th century.

Some of the words printed in *italics* may be new to you. You can look them up in the word list on page 92.

AN EYEWITNESS BOOK

Children of the Industrial Revolution

PENELOPE DAVIES

WAYLAND PUBLISHERS LONDON 1972

More Eyewitness Books

Frontispiece: Working children during the Industrial Revolution

First published 1972
Second impression 1975

SBN 85340 180 2
Copyright © 1972 by
Wayland Publishers Ltd
101 Grays Inn Road London WC1

Filmset by Keyspools Ltd, Golborne. Lancs.
Printed by Tinling (1973) Ltd, Prescot, Merseyside

Contents

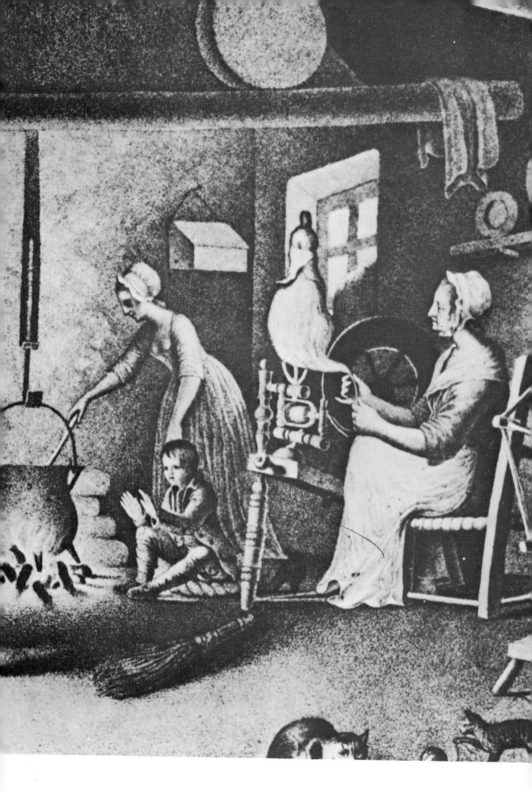

The Changing Countryside

One of the greatest changes that took place in Britain was the *Industrial Revolution.* Like so many periods in history, such as the Dark Ages or the Middle Ages, it had no definite beginning or ending. We cannot say that the Industrial Revolution began in 1790 and ended in 1850. Instead we have to say that England before about 1780–90 was mainly a farming country. But, by the middle of the nineteenth century, around 1845–60, farming was no longer the main industry. England had now become an industrial and manufacturing country. It is this great change that we call the Industrial Revolution.

Of course, there were industries in England centuries ago; but they were mostly quite small. In the north of the country, Newcastle exported coal from a few scattered pits as early as the year 1200. Coal mining was certainly an industry, but it was not large and took place in the country.

Before the Industrial Revolution England was a land of countryside with only a few towns. Most people lived in the country and earned their living from the land — either by farming, making farm tools, milling corn or doing other outside jobs. The few industries that did exist were what we call *cottage industries.* Instead of going out to work in factories, people worked at home. The Industrial Revolution helped change this England to the one we know today: big towns where most people work and live, and a much smaller amount of countryside where there are fewer people than ever before.

ENCLOSURES. About 200 years ago, farmers began to put fences around their fields so that they could keep more animals and make more money. Before these *enclosures* there was open land which everybody could use. Fewer people were needed to look after animals than to grow crops, and families had to travel all over the country looking for work.

THE WOODCUTTER'S SON. Today, with our dirty, noisy and crowded cities, it is nice to think of living and working in the country. But the country is not, and never has been, a place where the sun always shines, the birds always sing and everyone is happy. It was certainly not like this 200, or even 100 years ago. Most country people had to work very hard. How would you like to chop wood all day, sometimes in rain and snow? Many boys and girls had to, because selling wood was the only way their fathers could earn money.

LEECH COLLECTORS. Because work was hard to find people often had to do nasty jobs. Leech collecting was one. Leeches are small, blood-sucking creatures that live in water. The best way to collect them was to stand in a river or pond with bare legs. The leeches then came to suck the blood. As a cure for some illnesses, doctors used them to suck a sick person's "bad" blood, but often this only made the patient worse.

GLEANING. All country children helped their parents *glean* at harvest time. Harvesters had no machines to cut or bind the corn. Everything was done by hand. Because of this, quite a lot of corn was left behind, and the children had to collect what was left. The corn was ground into flour ready for their mother to make bread. The children got tired of picking up corn for hours at a time. But the parents knew that if the weather turned bad before they had finished gathering the harvest they would not have enough food to last the winter.

COTTAGE INDUSTRIES. The Industrial Revolution changed many industries, especially the cotton and woollen industries. Some of the great mills in Lancashire and Yorkshire are still in use today. Before the mills were built, most cotton and woollen goods were made at home. The two girls in the picture above use spinning wheels to make thread.

THE WOOLLEN INDUSTRY. In 1757, just before the Industrial Revolution, a writer called Josiah Tucker described the Yorkshire woollen industry: "Woollen making is carried on by small farmers. They buy some wool; their wives and daughters spin it at night, or when they are not working on the farm. The master of the family either sells this thread, or weaves it into cloth."

THE LITTLE SERVANT. Weavers who worked at home usually hired their *looms* for about five pence a week. You can see the loom at the back of this picture. The girl by the table is nine or ten years old. She has to look after the weaver's children, do the cooking, cleaning and washing. For this she earned about three pence a week.

POVERTY AND HUNGER. Illness for the poor meant no work, no money and no food. Sometimes an employer or his wife was kind and brought food. But this scene, described during George III's reign (1760—1820), was more usual: "A poor man, sick in bed, his ragged wife and children. A child came in with a loaf of bread. They all ran, snatched it and tore it in pieces at once."

T. Allom.

H. Robinson.

Mills, Mines and Factories

Before the Industrial Revolution, the British Isles was a land of farms and small industries, with most people living in the country. Why then in just fifty years, did it suddenly become full of mills, factories and offices, with people coming to live in towns and cities?

There are many reasons, but the main one was the improvement of the steam engine in the 1780's. Before, machines could only be worked by men, horses, water, or the weather. The wind blew the sails of a windmill, which worked the machinery grinding the corn. Water turned the wheels of the flour and silk mills. Horses drove the machines in breweries.

Steam engines were more powerful than anything else then known. They could drive bigger machines than those worked by men, and were much faster. Also, in the cotton and woollen industries, other new inventions, like the *spinning mule* and the *spinning jenny*, meant that more textiles could be made.

But all these new machines were expensive. They were also too big to fit into workers' homes. So the businessmen had to build factories or mills for the machines, and the people had to travel to work. Workers were easy to find, for the population was growing and many people had no jobs. The machines made many more goods than even the fastest workers, and so there was plenty to sell. It also meant that the goods were cheap to buy. More and more people bought the cheaper, factory-made products. Gradually, small businesses closed down, and people went to work in the new factories.

THE FIRST FACTORIES. Yorkshire had a woollen industry long before the Industrial Revolution. The industry went on, but in factories, not the workers' homes. This picture shows just one factory in about 1814. But the peaceful scene soon changed. The

hillside became covered with more factories and rows of rickety houses where the workers lived. The children had little time for play, and here they are on their way to work.

CARDING MACHINES. Factories were far more crowded and dirty than this picture shows. These machines are *carding* the wool before it is spun. The workers' clothes are very ragged. They had no time to make or mend them. One man told a Parliamentary Committee in 1831 that in the busiest times his three daughters (the youngest was only seven) worked from 3 a.m. to 10 p.m. They were paid 18p a week.

COLLECTING FLUFF. The huge machines in the picture above are spinning mules. They were used for winding up wool or cotton. Now you can see why one machine produced so much more than one man. Can you see the boy on the right? All day long he has to crawl under the machines picking up the cotton fluff. Before 1831 children usually worked from 6 a.m. to 8.30 p.m. Their lunch break was half an hour.

COTTON WORKERS. This is the winding room of a cotton mill. All the workers are children. Do you notice something else? They have nothing to sit on. Imagine standing from 6 a.m. to 7 p.m. with just forty minutes for lunch. On Saturdays children were luckier: in 1825 Parliament made a law that children should only work nine hours on a Saturday!

MAKING LINEN. These machines were used to make linen. A girl called Elizabeth Bentley worked in a Leeds flaxmill. In 1832 she told Parliament's Committee about her work: "I started working when I was six, usually from 6 a.m. to 7 p.m. If I was slow at my work I was beaten. The work was very dusty. The dust got on my lungs. My health got so bad that my bones became deformed."

TRAPPER BOYS. Children of six often worked down in the coal mines as *trappers*. They sat alone in the dark tunnels beside a wooden trap door for twelve hours a day. They had to open and shut the door to let coal trucks through. Lord Shaftesbury and other *reformers* tried to stop this. But some people said the work kept children out of mischief!

CHILD MINERS. In many of the coal mines children were needed more than grown-ups. Some of the tunnels were only 18 inches high, so children could crawl along them more easily than adults. A child usually worked twelve hours a day. One miner, John Bostock, said that he often fell asleep as he walked home from work.

WOMEN MINERS. In 1840 Parliament decided to find out about working conditions in the mines. One man told of "women and children chained and belted, harnessed like dogs in a go-cart, black, wet, half-naked crawling on their hands and feet, and dragging their heavy loads behind them."

MINE ACCIDENTS. Look at the pictures on the left. Every year at least two thousand people died in the mines. You can see in the picture above what will happen to the little girl on the lower rung of the ladder. Trapper boys were often killed. They went to sleep, fell on the track, and were run over by the heavy coal trucks. If the boy slipped when he was pulling a heavy cart, it ran back, killing or hurting the two boys behind.

LOST JOBS. It is terrible to think that women and children ever had to work in coal mines. But families were so poor that they all had to work to get enough money to live. However, Parliament's 1842 Mines Act put a stop to women and children working underground. In Scotland this caused great hardship as more than two thousand women lost their jobs. There was no other work, so many families were worse off.

BRICKMAKING. Work in the mines was dirty, heavy, and dangerous. But work above ground could be almost as bad. This picture, and the ones on the next two pages, show us what all children, and especially one little seven-year-old-boy, George Smith, had to do in brickyards. The two girls in this picture are sifting the dust before the bricks are made.

A BOY'S STORY. George Smith said: "I do not wish to say anything against my employer, but like many people then and even now (1871) he thought kicks and blows were the best way to make a child work. To these he added long hours. At nine years old, I had to carry forty pounds of clay on my head from one place to another. If there was no clay I had to carry bricks." In this picture you can see the children carrying clay.

LONG HOURS. After the child workers had collected their wages and gone home, it often took them days to get their strength back. George Smith tells us more about his work: "After one day's work I had to carry 1,200 nine-inch bricks from where they were made to where they were hardened. That night I walked fourteen miles. Altogether I carried $5\frac{1}{2}$ tons of clay. For this I was paid $2\frac{1}{2}$p. I was so tired after this that I could not work for some days."

DANGEROUS MACHINES. The two boys above are making ropes; the one below is working a cloth dyeing machine. Have a good look at these and the machines in the other pictures in this book. Can you see that they are all open? The moving parts are not covered. This was very dangerous and accidents often happened. One writer said that Manchester was so full of injured and crippled workers that it looked as if there had been a war.

HARD WORK AND BAD HEALTH. This cartoon was published to show people how badly children were treated in factories. Try and do this: stand with your left shoulder up and right knee bent in and your head bent down. Children in Bradford cloth factories had to stand like this twelve hours a day looking after machines. In 1831 it was reported that in Bradford alone more than 200 children were crippled by standing this way.

SCAVENGING. These factory children are hunting
for food in pig troughs. Their parents are too poor to
buy much food. Often, when the children did get
home they were too tired to eat. Seventeen-year-old
Joseph Hebergam told an inquiry, in 1831, that when
he was seven he worked from 5 a.m. to 8 p.m., with
half an hour at mid-day for a meal.

PUBLIC CONSCIENCE. Pictures such as this were used to show richer people what it was like to be a factory child. One man described it in 1818 as being: "Like a slave, locked up in factories eight storeys high, with no rest till the great machine stops, miserable food, mostly water gruel, oat-cake, a little salt, sometimes a little milk and a few potatoes."

Street Traders
and Family Businesses

Not all children worked in mines or factories. Before the Industrial Revolution, businesses had been small, with perhaps one or two families working together.

These small tradesmen did not make much money, or become rich, but they were independent. They lived and worked in poor, over-crowded little houses, but they could start and finish work when they wanted. But in factories, if a worker was ill or late, he was beaten and fined.

As time went, more machines were used, and many small firms had to close down. The huge amounts of cheap goods produced by the factories was too much for the smaller firms to compete with. This forced many people to find other work. It was not always easy. With thousands of men, women and children out of work, crime in industrial cities began to grow, and it was not until 1829 that England had its first proper police force.

In this chapter we will see how some children earned a living outside the factories. Perhaps you wonder why parents let their children work as chimney sweeps or in the coal mines. It is hard for us today to imagine how people could live on such low wages. A handloom weaver in 1830 earned 30p for working twelve hours a day, seven days a week. But no man could keep a family on this, so all members of the family had to help. As one man told Parliament's Committee in 1831: "Many said my son would be made a cripple (by factory work), but I am a poor man and could not afford to take him away."

COSTERMONGERS. Many city street sellers were *costermongers*. They sold fruit, vegetables and fish in the streets. One girl told the writer, Henry Mayhew, ''There's eight of us in family. Father did odd jobs, when work was slack we had very hard times. But my mother would buy a sack of apples to sell. We can earn $7\frac{1}{2}$p a day, sitting by the stall from 9 a.m. until the shops shut, about 10 p.m.

CRESS SELLER. "Fresh water cress! Fresh water cress!" This was one of the first sounds to be heard in city streets each morning. The cress sellers were mostly children. They bought the cress in the markets, before daylight. After tying the cress in halfpenny and penny bundles, they tramped round the streets trying to sell it. One little girl seller told Henry Mayhew she was "half past seven" ($7\frac{1}{2}$), but many others were even younger.

MATCH SELLERS. City streets rang with the cry:
"Buy a *fuzee* to light your pipe or cigar, sir! A row of
lights for a halfpenny!" Fuzees were cheap matches.
Poor people bought them from the makers for two-
pence a thousand. They sold them on the streets for
a halfpenny for twenty. Match sellers were some of
the poorest city children.

MATCH MAKERS. Here is another family at work. They are making match boxes. You can see all the boxes lying about. They probably earned about 3p for a thousand boxes. Notice that the window is patched with rags. The family cannot afford new glass. One father told Henry Mayhew that they never went out until evening, because their clothes were so ragged. But in the dark they didn't look so bad.

FAMILY OF TAILORS. Not all poor families earned their living in the streets. Here is a family at work making clothes. You can see a bed in the corner. They all lived and worked in this one room. But perhaps they are lucky. They do not live in a cellar. Families living in cellars near the Thames often had their homes flooded at high tide.

WATERMEN. When roads were bad and railways "new fangled" and frightening, river transport was important. But with the Industrial Revolution came steam driven boats. No one wanted the slow boats rowed by the *watermen*. As one said: "Last Friday I sat five hours before I earned a penny (less than $\frac{1}{2}$p)." Often these men slept under their boats. It was their only home.

CLIMBING BOYS. In the days before gas and electricity, chimneys often had to be cleaned because they got so full of soot. Children were used to sweep chimneys. In 1788 Parliament passed an Act to stop this. But no one took any notice. One rich lady declared she didn't mind what the law said, she liked boys cleaning her chimneys.

BECOMING A SWEEP. In 1817, during George III's reign (1760–1820), Parliament held an inquiry into the life and work of *climbing boys.* This is part of what they discovered: "Small boys are better, they can get up chimneys easier. Sweeps pay parents £2 or £3 for a boy of six. Boys are beaten and have pins stuck in their feet to make them climb. At first the knees, elbows and heels bleed all the time, but salt is rubbed in. This makes the skin hard."

CHIMNEY CLEANING BRUSH. In 1803 George Smart invented the Scandiscope brush to clean chimneys. As you can see from the picture on the right, it was made to fold up. This made it easier for the sweep to carry. On the left you can see it open. Rich ladies complained the brush made soot get all over the furniture. They never thought about the boys who cleaned the chimneys. Many boys got badly burnt and died. Others died from swallowing soot.

Within the banner:

TO EFFECT THE DELIVERANCE
FROM
PERSONAL SLAVERY
AND MORAL DEGRADATION OF THE
POOR CLIMBING BOYS
OF THE TOWN & COUNTY OF LEICESTER

1843 SWEEPS ACT. In 1843, during Queen Victoria's reign (1837–1901), a law was passed to stop children under ten years old working as sweeps. But there was nothing to stop poor parents lying about their child's age. If parents said a child was ten, no sweep was going to check. Gradually people began to realize how cruel this work was. The picture above shows a protest march that was held in Leicester. Later, in 1875, it was made illegal for all children to clean chimneys.

CROSSING SWEEPERS. A hundred years ago city streets were usually very dirty and not properly surfaced. The traffic was horse-drawn. In wet weather the mess was awful. Many poor children, and grown-ups as well, earned money as *crossing sweepers*. Their job was to sweep a clean path across the street in front of the richer people. If they were lucky they could earn nearly 5p a day.

CHILD CROSSING SWEEPERS. In the days when ladies wore long dresses, a clean path across the street helped keep hems clean. But one little girl, called Ellen, told Henry Mayhew that ladies never gave her as much money as gentlemen. Most of the children had no parents and many had no homes. Their clothes were dirty and torn and they were lucky if they wore shoes.

Down and Out

During the reign of Queen Victoria (1837–1901) London was one of the world's richest cities. Foreign visitors marvelled at the number of shops, theatres, and fine streets. But there was another side. A side very few of the people living in Portland Place or shopping in Regent Street knew about. It was the slums. All Britain's big industrial cities had them. All were terrible. Thousands of people were packed into tiny houses, with several families sharing a room. There were no drains, just the alleys between buildings. Crime, disease, violence, were all part of the every day life of the people living in such places. And it was the Industrial Revolution that was the cause.

In Chapter 1 we saw that before the Industrial Revolution most industries were small. In some cases each worker could work in his own home. But when people started to work in factories it meant they had to live near their work place as there was no public transport. The factories developed very fast. Workers needed houses. There was no time to plan and develop cities. The houses that were built were badly constructed and there were never enough to go round. So the slums grew up.

These figures show you just how fast English cities grew. The population of London was 960,000 in 1801. In 1851 it was nearly $2\frac{1}{2}$ million! In the same fifty years Leeds grew from 53,000 to 172,000 people. Bradford, a small town with 13,000 people, developed into a city of 104,000. Sheffield's population increased from 46,000 to 135,000 and Manchester's jumped from 90,000 to 400,000.

SLUMS. The pictures on the next few pages will show
you the way many poor townspeople had to live.
Don't forget that the lower classes, or "lower orders"
as they were usually called, were the largest part of
England's population at this time. One French tourist
remarked that two steps away from London's
wealthy streets lived children who were almost naked
and had figures like skeletons covered with rags.

SEVEN DIALS. Seven Dials in London, between Shaftesbury Avenue and Covent Garden, was a well-known centre of crime and violence. In the time of the author, Charles Dickens, it was even unsafe to go through the area in daylight. You can see how small the houses are. An Italian visitor in 1827 said jokingly that English people never waved their arms like Italians because there wasn't room in their tiny homes.

MANCHESTER. Other cities were as bad as London. This was Manchester in Victorian times (1850's). "The city seen close at hand is very dismal. The air and soil are full of fog and soot. Factories with blackened bricks stand in rows like prisons." But, as a rich factory owner said: "There is a great deal of money to be made in Manchester."

GLASGOW. This early photograph shows a Glasgow slum in 1870. But the houses were built much earlier. These houses had no water. An outside tap was shared by about twenty families. Lavatories as we know them did not exist. There was a smelly "privy" in the yard, which everyone shared. Windows were taxed until 1825, so the houses were dark. They smelt, too, because there weren't many windows to open.

WORKERS' HOMES. Diseases like cholera and typhus were common. Edwin Chadwick was one man who realized that bad living conditions and bad health were closely linked. He made a study for Parliament. He discovered that many Manchester workers only lived to be 17. In Leeds it was 19 and in Liverpool 15. But rich people usually lived to about 44 in Leeds and 35 in Liverpool.

COVENT GARDEN MARKET. Covent Garden was, and still is, London's fruit and vegetable market. It was also a good place for children to earn some money. They carried baskets, ran errands and stole food. Henry Mayhew, one of the few people really interested in London's poor, tells how boys slept at night in the big empty fruit baskets. And "on the steps of Covent Garden Theatre shoeless girls sit tying bundles of cress."

MUD LARKS. *Mud larks* were a common sight along the Thames at low tide. They were usually orphans or children from very poor families. They earned a little money by selling things they found on the mud. Coal sold at 14 lbs. for $\frac{1}{2}$p, iron at 5 lbs. a $\frac{1}{2}$p, 6 lbs. of bones fetched 1p. Often this was all they and their families had to live on.

STREET ARABS. Many of the slum children had no real homes. Instead they formed gangs and lived by stealing. One gang of boys made a cave on waste ground at Stratford, in east London, where they lived for some time. These wild children, nicknamed *"street arabs"*, often went to *ragged schools* (see Chapter 5). At these schools people were kind to them. Very few people in Victorian England were kind to street arabs.

PICKPOCKETS. Picking pockets was one way street children made a living. In his story, *Oliver Twist,* Charles Dickens tells us how boy *pickpockets* were trained by an old thief trainer. "They learn to be expert in this way: a coat is hung on the wall and a bell attached to it, and the boy has to take the handkerchief without ringing the bell."

A SUCCESSFUL PICKPOCKET. Henry Mayhew described a successful pickpocket: " . . . dressed in the latest fashion, glittering in gold chains, studs and rings." But a pickpocket who was caught faced heavy punishment. One man caught by the police in Cremorne, a London park, was sentenced to ten years imprisonment. He had stolen one handkerchief and some small change. In this picture you can see a pickpocket being taken away to prison in a wheelbarrow.

GAMBLING DEN. Gambling was a very popular pastime for thieves. Henry Mayhew describes one gambling den. "They meet in some secret place, about 10 a.m. and begin playing for $\frac{1}{2}$p stakes. Some cheat and some bet £50. The play lasts nearly all day. They never say a word when they are losing, they just stamp on the ground. When a man is losing leave him alone, he is dangerous."

SLEEPING ROUGH. Many townspeople had no homes. They had to sleep in the open. Patrick Colquhoun, a London magistrate, said that in 1818–1820 there were twenty thousand people without shelter. Lord Shaftesbury told the House of Commons in 1843 that he had found a homeless boy living inside a lawn roller in Regent's Park. London's bridges were the only bedrooms many people had.

PRISONS. Anyone caught committing a crime was harshly punished. Elizabeth Fry did much to reform English prisons. She describes Newgate Prison in 1814: "Nearly 300 women, sent there for every kind of crime, some not even tried, kept in two small rooms and two cells. They all sleep on the floor without bedding. In all this horror were some 70 children." Here is a picture of a prison at the time of the Industrial Revolution.

PRISON REFORMS. This picture shows the changes that Mrs. Fry and other prison reformers made. Women prisoners now had women warders to look after them. They were given work to do and taught to look after themselves and their children. But change was slow. London's Pentonville Prison, which was opened in 1842, was criticized by many people. They thought it too good for the prisoners because each one had a cell with a bed.

CHILD PRISONERS. It was quite legal to send children to prison. They were imprisoned with older criminals, who taught them even more about crime. Mary Carpenter, another reformer, realized this was bad. In December, 1851, a conference in Birmingham decided to set up special reform schools. Children were sent to these instead of prison. At the schools they learnt a trade to help them make money honestly.

Reforms and Reformers

Today we wonder how any factory owner could ever have let children do such awful work. But not all were cruel. Robert Peel and Robert Owen tried hard to make working places better, and Lord Shaftesbury, the greatest of all reformers, made many enemies in his efforts to help working children.

Why was factory life so bad and changes so slow? Mainly because wealthy people were afraid of change. In the time of the Industrial Revolution Britain was divided much more sharply between rich and poor. The middle class was small, compared with today. The rich people did not have to work, and many really believed that the poor were there to work for them. Children were paid less than grown-ups. If children were not allowed to work, the factory owners would have to pay more wages and make less money. So naturally, they didn't want change.

We must also realize that many good people could not see anything wrong in making children work. It was thanks to the work of William Wilberforce that the slave trade was stopped. But Wilberforce had many children working in his factories. They were not called slaves, but that is what they really were. Wilberforce did not think this was cruel. Bread was the main food of the poor and Robert Peel (junior) worked hard to make it cheaper. But, he opposed all efforts to shorten children's working hours.

Men like these were not bad, they had blind spots, but so does everyone. The reformers were men less blind than most people of their time.

THE RICH AND THE POOR. This picture was published in 1839. It shows what many rich people thought about the poor. The smartly dressed men are saying to the lady "Gracious Heaven, you are not going to speak to those creatures, Miss Brotherton?" Reformers had to try to change this kind of behaviour, but it was a long, slow job.

REFORMS. As early as the 1800s a few factory owners realized how bad conditions were for working children. But most people were against reforms or improvements. Not until about 30 years later did feeling begin to change. Cartoons, like this one from the magazine *Punch* in 1843, helped. The life of the rich, idle mine owner and his wife is compared with that of the poor labourers.

SIR ROBERT PEEL. One early reformer was Sir Robert Peel, M.P. He saw how hard the mill children had to work and how unhealthy they looked. To improve their working hours he got a law passed by Parliament in 1802. The law made it illegal for children to work at night and to work for more than twelve hours a day. Many people disobeyed this law, but it was a step in the right direction.

ROBERT OWEN. The Scottish mill owner, Robert Owen (1771–1858), was one industrialist who treated his workers well. He built a village for them near his factory. He made sure the children did not work too long. These things made Owen unpopular with other factory owners. Many people believed that England's trade would suffer if children worked shorter hours.

NEW LANARK. These are Robert Owen's cotton mills at New Lanark, Scotland. He looked after his workers well, giving them shops, decent housing and working conditions. The New Lanark mills were very successful and made lots of money. This made him even more unpopular with businessmen who did not agree with his "cranky" ideas about treating workers.

FACTORY SCHOOL. All the children at New Lanark went to school. Owen believed that everyone should be educated. As well as reading and writing, the children danced and played games, which was something very few working children ever did. Reformers from all over England and Europe visited New Lanark. This helped to spread new ideas about reform.

BOOKS ABOUT REFORM. Robert Owen wrote books to spread his ideas. These two pictures show that he knew what a poor background and homelife did to people. Not many people realized this. It is easy to be honest if you always have plenty to eat. But if you are hungry and have no money, stealing seems an easy answer.

LORD SHAFTESBURY. Lord Shaftesbury (1801–1885) was probably this country's greatest reformer. All his life he tried to help working children. He had a Factory Act passed in 1833. Children under nine years old could not work. Children between nine and thirteen must only work eight hours a day. Those under eighteen were limited to twelve hours each day. Mill owners who disobeyed this law were punished.

LORD SHAFTESBURY AND THE MINES. In 1840 Lord Shaftesbury got Parliament to hold an Inquiry about children working in the mines. He went down pits to see what they were really like. Here he sees a boy chained to a coal truck to pull it along. The rich mine owners did not like Shaftesbury showing them up.

MINES ACT, 1842. The Inquiry's report was published in 1842. It was illustrated and this picture comes from the report. For the first time people saw the mines as they really were. The Mines Act was quickly passed. It stated that no child under ten could work in the mines, and that women and girls must not work underground. The mines would also be inspected to see that this law was being obeyed.

LORD SHAFTESBURY AND RAGGED SCHOOLS.

Factory and mine children were not the only ones who needed help. In 1843 Lord Shaftesbury saw an advertisement in the newspaper *The Times* for help in a "ragged school". He went to the school. It was in a rough part of Holborn, London: "I saw thirty or forty men and boys, none with shoes and socks and some with no shirts. Wild and rough but listening to the teacher."

JOHN POUNDS. Ragged schools were not new in Victorian England. They started in Portsmouth around 1790. John Pounds, a cobbler, took in poor, ragged children who had no homes or families. He taught them to read and write. He also showed them how to cook their food and mend their clothes.

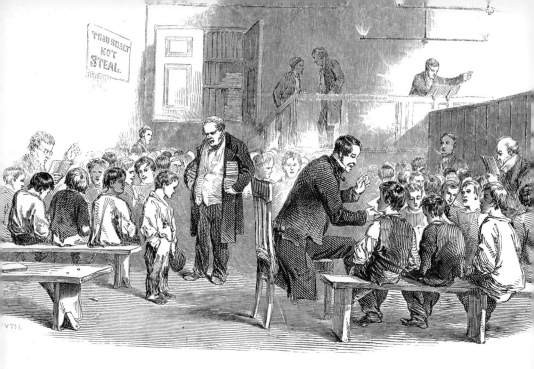

RAGGED AND INDUSTRIAL SCHOOLS. Other people copied John Pounds and soon there were ragged schools all over the country. All the teachers were volunteers. The children paid nothing. They couldn't pay, they had no money. Reading and writing were not the only subjects taught. Many of the schools were called Ragged and Industrial Schools. At these the children learnt simple trades, so they could get jobs and earn money.

PUNISHMENTS FOR CHILDREN. Ragged schools helped to keep poor children out of trouble. Why? Because they were cold and hungry they often stole things. This made people dislike poor children. They were harshly punished for doing anything wrong. In 1833 a boy of nine was hung for stealing paint worth 1p. Eleven years later, an eight-year-old boy was whipped and imprisoned for a month for stealing.

CHARLES DICKENS. Charles Dickens (1812–1870) was another reformer. He wrote books and articles in newspapers. His stories, like *Oliver Twist* and *Nicholas Nickleby*, were written to show people how awful some children's lives were. He did not like the ragged schools. He thought that they taught too much religion. He called Lord Shaftesbury "a friendly bull in a china shop of good intentions."

SUNDAY SCHOOLS. Sunday schools were started during George III's reign (1760–1820) by Robert Raikes in Gloucester. He wanted factory children to have some education and Sunday was their only free day. The richer people thought religion very important. So Sunday schools taught more religion than reading or writing. But it was a start. When Richard Arkwright built a new factory he also built a church and school, where the child workers went each Sunday.

CHARITY SCHOOLS. Some of the first schools for the poor were run by charities. The Quakers had several schools. This one was in Gravel Lane, London. Charity schools had little money and teachers were hard to find. But there were other problems. School inspectors reported bad attendance. Children also had to leave classes to take meals to their families in the factories.

SCHOOLS. Many children hated going to school. It was almost as bad as working in the factories. Parents disliked school too, because the children didn't earn money there. The teachers were often cruel, and girls as well as boys were often beaten. One inspector reported that he saw whole classes hit and beaten even when they had done nothing wrong.

MORE REFORMS. Gradually more people tried to do something about education for the poor. The picture below is a school for blind people at St. George's Fields, Southwark, London, which was opened in 1799. Education also became available for the poor. The 1833 Factory Act said that all children between nine and thirteen must have two hours teaching a day. This wasn't much, but it was a beginning.

IMPROVEMENTS IN HOUSING. Look at the pictures on the right. People also began to think that the "lower orders" should not have to live in such cramped conditions like these shown in the picture above. In 1844, the "Society for improving the conditions of the labouring classes" studied London's housing problem. In what is now London's smart West End, they found 1,465 families living in 2,174 rooms! To try to improve things, the Society built houses like these model houses in the picture opposite.

SOUP KITCHENS. This picture shows one way the poor could be helped. Here is a *soup kitchen* in London's East End. At the beginning of the Industrial Revolution it was believed that only lazy people did not work. So, if they were poor it was their fault. It took many years before well-off people understood that sometimes there is not enough work for everybody.

Table of Dates

1760	George III comes to the throne
1764	James Hargreaves designs the spinning jenny
1780's	James Watt improves steam engine
1788	Unsuccessful act to stop the use of children as chimney sweeps
1790's	Ragged Schools started
1802	Factory Act reduced children's hours to twelve a day, and stopped nightwork
1805	Battle of Trafalgar
1815	Battle of Waterloo
1819	"Battle of Peterloo" in Manchester— women and children massacred by soldiers
1820	Death of George III. George IV becomes king
1825	First passenger railway opened, from Stockton-on-Tees to Darlington
1829	Britain's first professional police force started in London
1832	The Great Reform Act
1833	Factory Act. Children under nine no longer work in factories
1837	Queen Victoria comes to the throne
1842	Mines Act. No girl, woman or boy under ten to work underground
1843	Sweeps Act. No child under ten to work as a sweep
1846	Repeal of the Corn Laws cuts the price of bread
1870	Education Act makes all children from five to twelve go to school

New Words

Carding Machine	Machine that prepared wool before it was spun into thread
Climbing Boys	Another name for chimney sweeps
Costermonger	A person selling fruit, fish or vegetables in the street
Cottage Industries	Industry in which the workers worked in their own homes
Crossing Sweeper	Someone who swept a clean path across the street for pedestrians
Enclosures	Fencing in of farm land for grazing animals
Fuzee	Cheap matches sold in the streets by match sellers
Glean	To collect corn that is dropped by harvesters
Industrial Revolution	Period roughly from 1780–1850. Britain changed from a farming country to a manufacturing country
Loom	Machine for weaving cloth
Mudlarks	Children who searched river mudbanks for things to sell
Pickpocket	Someone who steals from people's pockets

Ragged Schools	Elementary schools, run by charities, for poor children
Reformer	Someone who tried to improve the lives of poor people
Soup Kitchen	Place where poor people got free food
Spinning Jenny	Machine for spinning many threads at once
Spinning Mule	A machine for twisting and winding wool or cotton
Street Arabs	Homeless children who lived in the streets
Trappers	Small children who worked the trap doors in coal mines
Watermen	Boatmen who rowed people or goods across or along rivers

More Books

Cookson, C. *The Nipper* (Macdonald, 1970). The adventures of a small boy who worked in coal-mines and on farms.

Dickens, C. *David Copperfield* (Collins, 1971). An abridged edition with plenty of illustrations. For older readers.

Hart, R. W. *English Life in the Eighteenth Century* (Wayland, 1970). A well illustrated survey of the century, with a good section on the Industrial Revolution. For older readers.

Hennessey, R. A. S. *Factories* (Batsford, 1969). The first part of this book deals with the development and growth of industrial Britain. Best for older readers.

Lovett, M. *Jonathan* (Faber, 1972). The adventures of an orphan family, set against the mills, mines and potteries.

Quennell, M. and C. H. B. *History of Everyday Things in England, Vol. III* (Batsford, 1967). Clear, simple and illustrated accounts of many of the inventions made during the Industrial Revolution.

Rooke, P. *The Age of Dickens* (Wayland, 1970). A well illustrated and documented view of Britain during the life of a great writer and reformer. For older readers.

The Industrial Revolution covered the reigns of George III (1760–1820), George IV (1820–1830), William IV (1830–1837) and the beginning of Queen Victoria's rule (1837–1891). So you will find that many books on Georgian, Regency and Victorian Britain have sections on the Industrial Revolution.

Index

Picture Credits

The Publishers wish to thank the following for their kind permission to reproduce copyright illustrations on the pages mentioned: Mansell Collection, jacket, frontispiece, 11, 14, 15, 16, 18–19, 20, 21, 23, 29, 30, 34, 35, 36, 41, 55, 60, 65, 67, 68, 70, 71, 72, 73, 74, 75, 76, 77, 78, 80, 81, 83, 87, 89, 90; Radio-Times Hulton Picture Library, 6, 12, 13, 22, 26 (top), 27, 32 (top), 44, 49, 50, 52, 79, 85, 88 (bottom); Mary Evans Picture Library, 24, 25, 28, 31, 33, 38, 42, 47, 48, 53, 59, 61, 62, 63, 66, 82; Trustees of the London Museum, 56; Trustees of the British Museum, 64; Trustees of the National Portrait Gallery, 84. Other illustrations appearing in this book are the property of the Wayland Picture Library.